BUT LISTEN TO ME; FOR ONE MOMENT, QUIT BEING SAD. HEAR BLESSINGS DROPPING THEIR BLOSSOMS AROUND YOU.

THE POETRY:

Rumi was born in Balkh, Afghanistan, then part of the Persian empire, in 1207. Fleeing the threat of invading Mongol armies, his family emigrated to Konya, Turkey, a city where Muslim, Christian, Hindu and Buddhist travelers mingled. There Rumi

A   J O U R N A L

studied with his father to be a religious scholar. Then Rumi met a wandering dervish named Shams of Tabriz, who became his teacher and spiritual companion. Their meeting altered the course of Rumi's life—and thus our lives today. Rumi's passionate, playful poems help us celebrate the sacredness of everyday life and glimpse its deepest mysteries. As Rumi writes in one of his poems, *"create your own myth."*

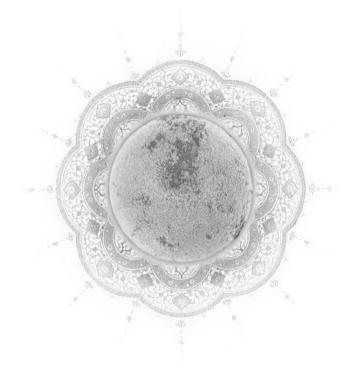

Though we seem to be sleeping,
there is an inner wakefulness
that directs the dream,
and that will eventually startle us back
to the truth of who we are.

Days full of wanting.
Let them go by without worrying
that they do. Stay where you are
inside such a pure, hollow note.

Observe the wonders as they occur around you.
Don't claim them. Feel the artistry
moving through, and be silent.

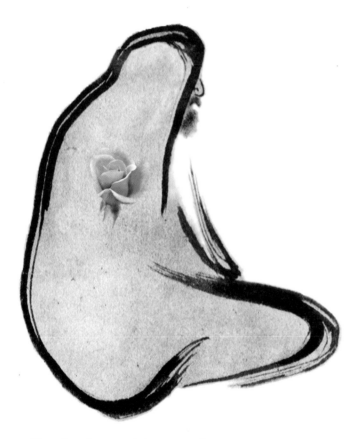

Keep knocking, and the joy inside
will eventually open a window
and look to see who's there.

Whoever acts with respect will get respect.
Whoever brings sweetness
will be served almond cake.

I can't explain the goings,
or the comings. You enter suddenly,
and I am nowhere again.
Inside the majesty.

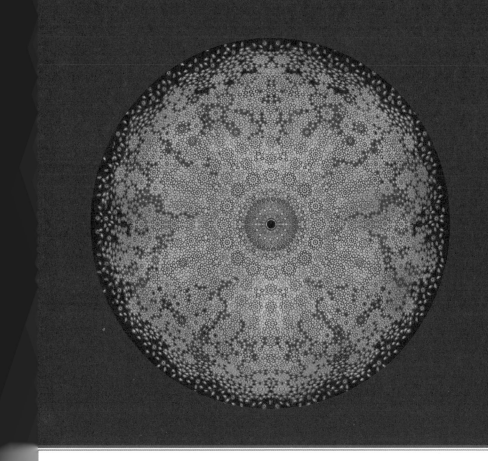

power means nothing. Only the unsayable,
inner life matters.

This is not a day for asking questions,
not a day on any calendar.
This day is conscious of itself.
This day is a lover, bread, and gentleness,
more manifest than saying can say.

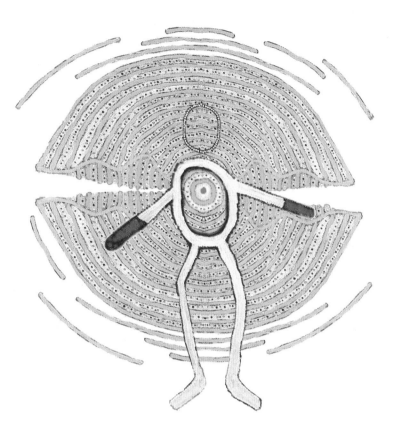

There is a community of the spirit
Join it, and feel the delight
of walking in the noisy street,
and being the noise.

Close both eyes
to see with the other eye.

Be empty of worrying.
Think of who created thought!

Why do you stay in prison
when the door is so wide open?

You must have shadow and light source both.
Listen, and lay your head under the tree of awe.

Your way begins on the other side.
Become the sky.
Take an axe to the prison wall.
Escape.
Walk out like someone suddenly born into color.
Do it now.

Stop the words now.
Open the window in the center of your chest,
and let spirit fly in and out.

Unfold your own myth.

What is love?
Gratitude.

What is hidden
in our chests?
Laughter.

What else?
Compassion.

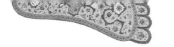

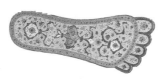

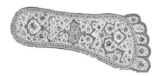

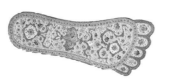

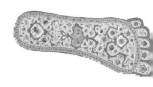

Be grateful for whoever comes,
because each has been sent
as a guide from beyond.

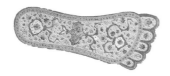

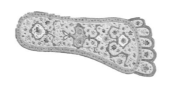

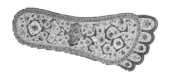

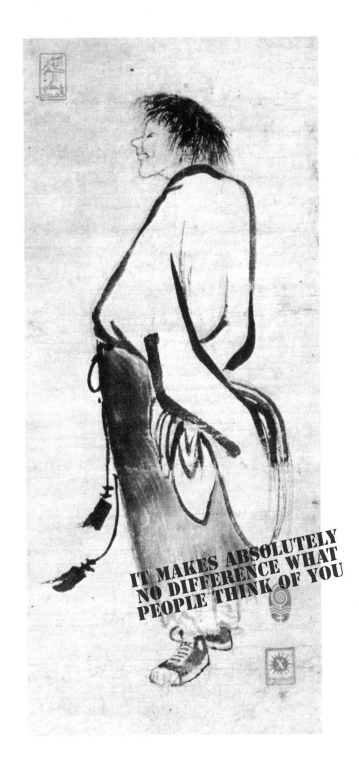

IT MAKES ABSOLUTELY
NO DIFFERENCE WHAT
PEOPLE THINK OF YOU

Whoever finds love
beneath hurt and grief

disappears into emptiness
with a thousand new disguises.

But what can stay hidden?
Love's secret is always lifting its head
out from under the covers,
"Here I am!"

A great silence overcomes me,
and I wonder why I ever thought
to use language.

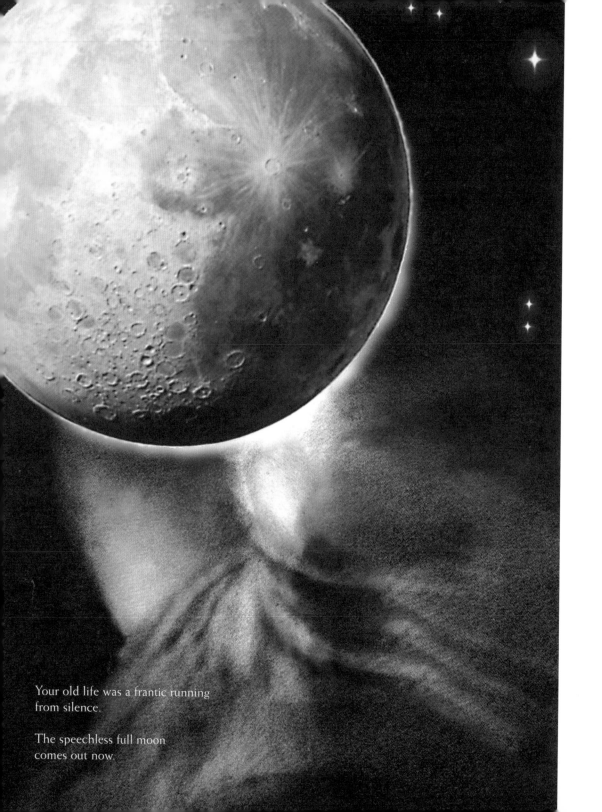

Your old life was a frantic running
from silence.

The speechless full moon
comes out now.

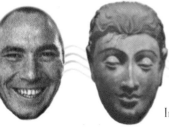

Instead of being so bound up with everyone,
Be everyone.

Everything has to do with loving and not loving.
This night will pass.
Then we have work to do.

Pale sunlight,
pale the wall.

Love moves away.
the light changes.

I need more grace
than I thought.

Awe is the salve
that will heal our eyes.

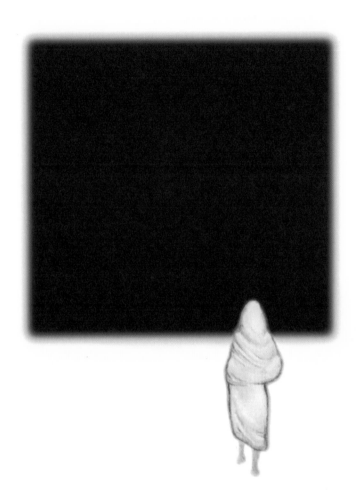

Which is worth more, a crowd of thousands,
or your own genuine solitude?
Freedom, or power over an entire nation.

A little while alone in your room
will prove more valuable than anything else
that could ever be given you.

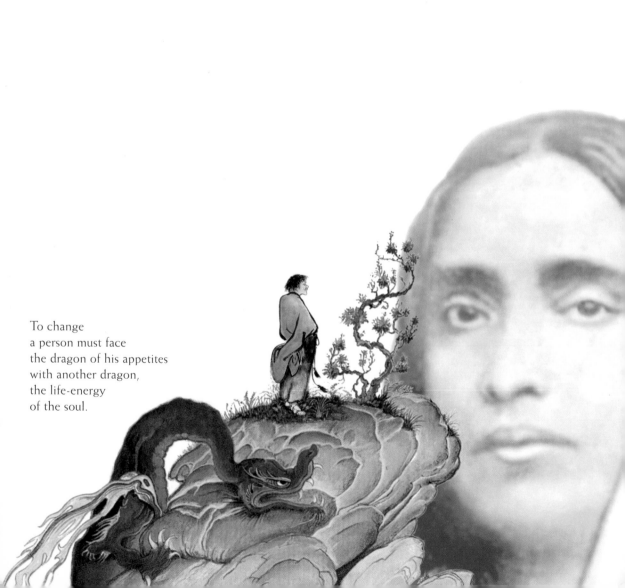

To change
a person must face
the dragon of his appetites
with another dragon,
the life-energy
of the soul.

Every part of you has a secret language.
Your hands and your feet say what you've done.
And every need brings in what's needed.
Pain bears its cure like a child.
Having nothing produces provisions.
Ask a difficult question,
and the marvelous answer appears.

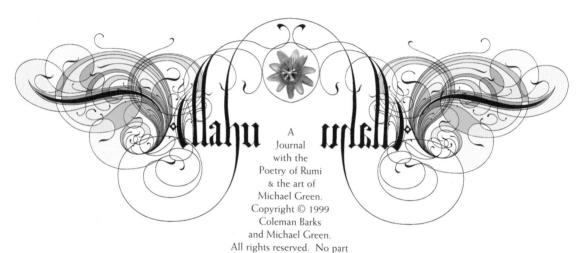

A
Journal
with the
Poetry of Rumi
& the art of
Michael Green.
Copyright © 1999
Coleman Barks
and Michael Green.
All rights reserved. No part
of this book may be reproduced or transmitted in any
form or by any means, electronic or mechanical, including photocopying, recording, or by any
information storage and retrieval system, without written permission from the publisher. Entire book designed by Michael Green.

Rumi is the 13th Century Sufi mystic, whose ability to open the heart so dissolved the boundaries of religion that he made human friendship and the longing to merge with the Source one thing. His spontaneously spoken poetry celebrates the sacredness of every-day life and gives voice to the soul's deepest mysteries. On page 119 are the hands of a contemporary Sufi master, Bawa Muhaiyaddeen.
Coleman Barks has published twelve books of Rumi's poetry, including the best-selling THE ESSENTIAL RUMI. He lives in Athens Georgia and is a professor at the University of Georgia. A catalogue of his books is available at 1800-682-8637.
Michael Green is a critically acclaimed artist and illustrator whose books include THE ILLUMINATED RUMI, ZEN AND THE ART OF THE MACINTOSH, UNICORNIS, THE BOOK OF DRAGONTOOTH, and THE I-CHING RECORDS. He lives in Pennsylvania's Brandywine Valley.
Much of the art in this book is available in fine-art prints at rumiarts.com

Brush Dance

The *Brush Dance* is a Yurok Indian healing ritual where being true to yourself means giving your best to help a person in need.
Being true to yourself is the one and only Yurok Indian law.

For more information about Brush Dance, or to find our where to purchase our cards, journals and other products, contact us at
165 N. Redwoods Drive, Suite 200, San Rafael, CA 94903 • (800) 531-7445 • www.brushdance.com • Printed in Korea